Why Vietnamese Immigrants Came to America

Lewis K. Parker

The Rosen Publishing Group's
PowerKids Press™
New York

Published in 2003 by The Rosen Publishing Group, Inc.
29 East 21st Street, New York, NY 10010

First Edition

Book Design: Mindy Liu and Erica Clendening

Photo Credits: Cover © AFP/Corbis; p. 4 Lee Lockwood/TimePix; pp. 5, 20 © MapArt; pp. 6–7, 10, 11, 12, 13, 21 (top) © AP/Wide World Photos; pp. 6 (inset), 8–9, Still Picture Branch, National Archives and Record Administration; p. 15 © Alan Levenson/TimePix; p. 16 © Ted Thai/TimePix; pp. 17, 21 (bottom) © Catherine Karnow/Corbis; p. 19 © Oak Ridge National Laboratory, photo by Curtis Boles

Library of Congress Cataloging-in-Publication Data

Parker, Lewis K.
Why Vietnamese immigrants came to America / Lewis K. Parker.
    p. cm. — (Coming to America)
Summary: Explores Vietnamese immigration to the United States from the 1960s to the present, and looks at the contributions of Vietnamese Americans to the culture of the United States.
Includes bibliographical references and index.
ISBN 0-8239-6461-2 (lib. bdg.)
1. Vietnamese Americans—History—Juvenile literature. 2. Immigrants—United States—History—Juvenile literature. 3. Refugees—Vietnam—History—Juvenile literature. 4. Refugees—United States—History—Juvenile literature. 5. United States—Emigration and immigration—History—Juvenile literature. 6. Vietnam—Emigration and immigration—History—Juvenile literature. [1. Vietnamese Americans—History. 2. Immigrants—History. 3. Refugees—Vietnam. 4. Vietnam—Emigration and immigration. 5. United States—Emigration and immigration.] I. Title.
E184.V53 P37 2003
304.8'730597—dc21

                                        2002000162

North Vietnam wanted to take over South Vietnam. In 1955, a war started between North Vietnam and South Vietnam.

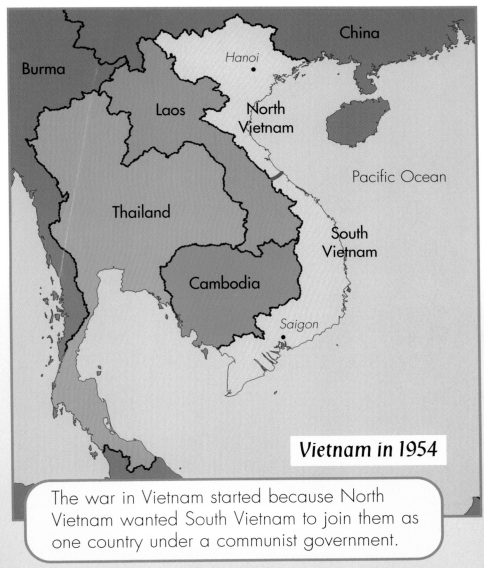

Vietnam in 1954

The war in Vietnam started because North Vietnam wanted South Vietnam to join them as one country under a communist government.

The Vietnam War made life hard for the people of North and South Vietnam. Villages and cities were destroyed. Over three million people living in Vietnam were killed.

During the Vietnam War, about 58,000 American soldiers were killed in Vietnam.

By 1962, the United States had sent about 11,000 soldiers to South Vietnam. Their job was to help stop North Vietnam from taking over South Vietnam.

The Vietnam War ended in 1975. North Vietnam won the war. North and South Vietnam became one country with a communist government. Vietnam was a poor country. Millions of people had lost their homes, jobs, and businesses.

Many buildings and homes in Vietnam were destroyed during the war.

The Fact Box

When the Vietnam War ended, more than ten million people were homeless.

9

Leaving Home

After the war, over 200,000 people left Vietnam to find a better life. Many of these people escaped from Vietnam in small boats and sailed to nearby countries. From those countries, most of the Vietnamese people traveled to America on boats or planes. The trip out of Vietnam was dangerous and many people died.

Many people who left Vietnam were called "boat people" because they had to travel on crowded boats.

"My mother was hesitant to get on board [the boat] because she had to choose between leaving us or staying to see her mother for the first time since 1954. As the boat pulled away, I can still remember my mother standing on the dock, crying and waving to us."

— Darlene Nguyen Ely, who immigrated in 1975

Life in America

When the Vietnamese immigrants came to America, they sometimes stayed in army camps where they learned how to speak and read English. They also learned about life in America.

U.S. soliders helped Vietnamese people leave their war-torn country.

After arriving in America, many Vietnamese immigrants went to U.S. army bases.

The new life in the United States was not easy for Vietnamese immigrants. Many Americans helped the immigrants by giving them housing, food, and clothing.

Many Vietnamese immigrants worked hard at low-paying jobs. They saved their money and sent their children to college.

Many Vietnamese immigrants moved to large cities where they could find work. Others moved to coastal areas and worked as fishermen. Like other immigrant groups, Vietnamese people often lived near one another in small communities.

Many Vietnamese immigrants made their living as fishermen.

Vietnamese immigrants set up Little Saigon, a community near Los Angeles. More than 200,000 Vietnamese Americans now live in Little Saigon.

Vietnamese Immigrants Today

Most Vietnamese immigrants have only been in the United States for about 25 years. Many have started their own businesses, such as restaurants and jewelry shops. Others have become lawyers, doctors, teachers, and scientists. Each year, thousands of Vietnamese immigrants still come to America for a better way of life.

Tuan Vo-Dinh is a Vietnamese immigrant who has become a successful scientist. He invented an important machine for testing blood.

Between 1990 and 2000, the number of Vietnamese people in the United States almost doubled. Today, about 1.2 million Vietnamese people live in the United States. The Vietnamese, many of whom escaped their small, war-torn country, are helping to make America successful.

Cities with Large Numbers of Vietnamese Americans

United States

San Francisco/
San Jose
147,000

Washington, D.C.
44,000 ★

Los Angeles
★ 234,000

Dallas/
Fort Worth
47,000

Houston/
Galveston
64,000

Atlantic
Ocean

Pacific
Ocean

Vietnamese people celebrate Tet, the Vietnamese New Year, at the end of January or early February.

Many Vietnamese immigrants have made a new life for themselves in America.

Glossary

coastal (**koh**-stuhl) having to do with land that is next to the sea or ocean

college (**kahl**-ihj) a school where people can study after high school

communism (**kahm**-yuh-nihz-uhm) a type of government that controls people's jobs and everything they own

communist (**kahm**-yuh-nihzt) supporter of the idea of communism

community (kuh-**myoo**-nuh-tee) a group of people living in the same place; the place where they live

immigrant (**ihm**-ih-grunt) someone who comes into a country to live there

paddy (**pad**-ee) a wet field where rice is grown

restaurants (**rehs**-tuh-rahnts) places to buy and eat a meal

separated (**sehp**-uh-ray-tuhd) keeping two things apart; divided

Vietnam War (vee-eht-**nahm wor**) battles from 1955–1975 in which the South Vietnamese people, with help from American soldiers starting in 1962, fought communists from North Vietnam

Resources

Books

Vietnam: The Boat People Search for a Home
by John Isaac and Keith Elliot Greenberg
Blackbirch Marketing (1996)

Two Lands, One Heart: An American Boy's Journey to His Mother's Vietnam
by Jeremy Schmidt
Walker and Company (1995)

Web Sites

Due to the changing nature of Internet links, PowerKids Press has developed an online list of Web sites related to the subjects of this book. This site is updated regularly. Please use this link to access the list:

http://www.powerkidslinks.com/cta/vie/

Index

C

communist government,
  4–5, 8

community, 16–17

I

immigrant, 12–19, 21

J

jewelry, 18

R

restaurants, 18

S

separated, 4

soldiers, 6–7

V

Vietnam, 4–6, 8, 10

Vietnam War, 4, 6,
  8–9

Word Count: 399

Note to Librarians, Teachers, and Parents

If reading is a challenge, Reading Power is a solution! Reading Power is perfect for readers who want high-interest subject matter at an accessible reading level. These fact-filled, photo-illustrated books are designed for readers who want straightforward vocabulary, engaging topics, and a manageable reading experience. With clear picture/text correspondence, leveled Reading Power books put the reader in charge. Now readers have the power to get the information they want and the skills they need in a user-friendly format.

Crafts to Celebrate

God's Creation

Crafts
to Celebrate
God's
Creation

By Kathy Ross
Illustrated by Sharon Lane Holm

Christian Crafts
The Millbrook Press
Brookfield, Connecticut

To my loving and supportive extended family
at Gethsemane Church, Sherrill, NY
K.R.

For Pat and Merial, thank you!
S.L.H.

With special thanks to Patti M. Hummel and the Benchmark Group

Library of Congress Cataloging-in-Publication data
Ross, Kathy.
Crafts to celebrate God's creation/by Kathy Ross; illustrated by Sharon Lane Holm.
p. cm.
ISBN 0-7613-1621-3 (lib. bdg.) ISBN 0-7613-1330-3 (pbk.)
1. Bible crafts--Juvenile literature. 2. Creation--Study and teaching (Primary)--Activity
programs--Juvenile literature. 3. Christian education--Activity programs--Juvenile
literature. [1. Bible crafts. 2. Handicraft. 3. Creation.] I. Holm, Sharon Lane, ill. II. Title.
BS613 .R69 2001
268'.432--dc21   00-039413

Published by The Millbrook Press, Inc.
2 Old New Milford Road
Brookfield, Connecticut 06804
www.millbrookpress.com

3 Cut a 1 1/2-inch (3.75-cm) circle from the yellow construction paper. This will be the moon. Glue it in the night sky, making sure it will be visible through the window cut in the top plate. Glue sticker stars around the moon. Use glue, even though the stars are self-stick, so that they will not rub off when turning the sky from night to day.

4 Cut a 2-inch (5-cm) circle from the yellow paper for the sun. Glue the sun on the blue-sky portion of the plate, making sure it will be visible through the window cut in the top plate. Glue some wisps of fiberfill over one side of the sun for the clouds.

5 Paint around the window with poster paint for the walls. Paint a floor below the window using a different color paint.

6 Use the yarn, doilies, and other collage materials to decorate the "room."

7 Place the window plate over the sky plate and fasten them together with a paper fastener through the center of the two plates.

To change the night to day, just turn the back plate around to show the day sky.

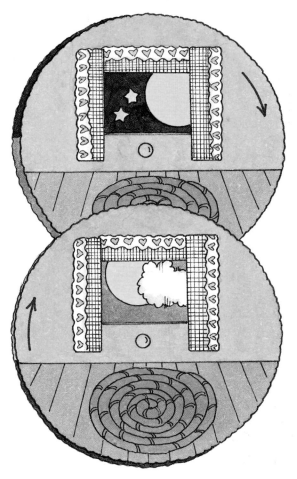

Thank you, God, for the night to rest and the day to learn more about your love.

God put the sky over the earth.

Sky Puppet

brown lunch bag

blue and green poster paints and a paintbrush

white glue

fiberfill

Seed catalog

seed catalog

scissors

what you do:

1 Work with the bag upside-down and the folded bottom of the bag on top.

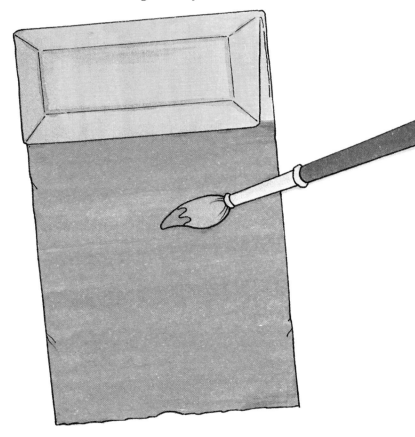

2 Paint the part of the bag below the edge of the bag bottom green for the grass.

4 Staple the filter to the cup.

5 Paint the Styrofoam ball yellow for the sun. Cut 3/4-inch (2-cm)- long pieces of orange pipe cleaner to stick around the ball for the rays of the sun.

6 Push the craft stick into the bottom of the sun. Pull the stick out, cover the end with glue, and put it back in.

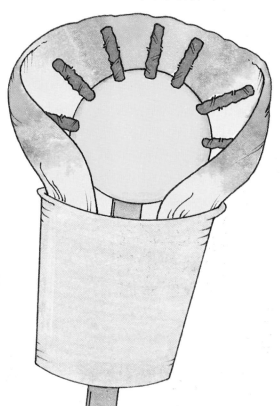

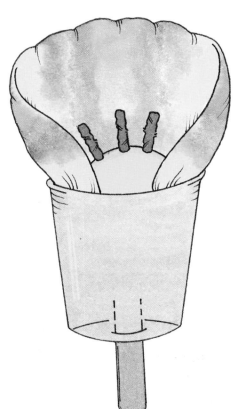

7

Poke a hole through the bottom of the cup. Drop the end of the craft stick down through the hole so that the sun is hidden in the cup and only the beautiful colors of the sky above the horizon are visible.

You can make your sun rise by pushing on the end of the stick at the bottom of the cup.

Thank you, God, for the sun that comes up every morning.

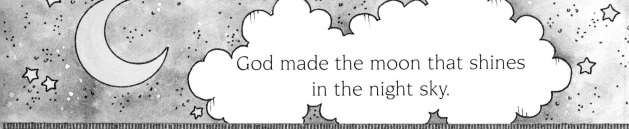

God made the moon that shines
in the night sky.

The Changing Moon

round lid from
a cookie tin

yellow tissue
paper

pencil

ribbon

white glue

masking tape

black
construction
paper

sticky-back
magnet strip

scissors

what you do:

1 Use the pencil to trace around the lid on the yellow tissue paper. Cut the traced circle out. Glue the circle inside the lid for the moon.

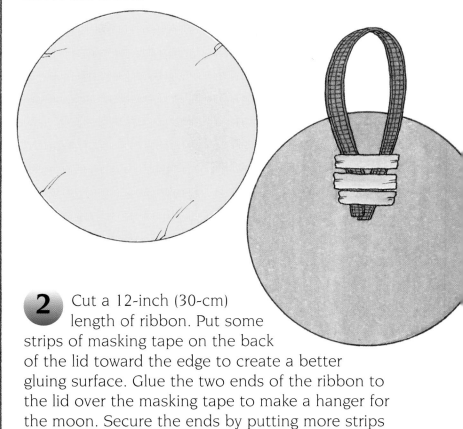

2 Cut a 12-inch (30-cm) length of ribbon. Put some strips of masking tape on the back of the lid toward the edge to create a better gluing surface. Glue the two ends of the ribbon to the lid over the masking tape to make a hanger for the moon. Secure the ends by putting more strips of masking tape over them.

3 The size of the moon changes as it goes through a cycle. It goes from being completely covered by the earth's shadow to a full circle, then gets smaller and smaller again until it is gone from view. Use the pencil to trace around the lid on the black paper. Cut out three black circles. Leave one circle whole to completely cover the moon. Put a piece of sticky-back magnet on the back of the circle. Cut another circle in half and put a piece of magnet on the back of one half. Cut a sliver of circle from the last circle and put a piece of magnet on the back of each piece.

Watch the moon each night as it goes from a full yellow circle to nothing and back to a full circle again. As the moon gets smaller, you can shadow the right side of your own moon model with more and more black paper. As it gets bigger again, turn the shadows around to shadow less and less of the left side of the moon. You can make lots more shadows in between these sizes or just change the shadow on your moon every few days as you notice a similar change in the size of the moon. What an amazing plan God has!

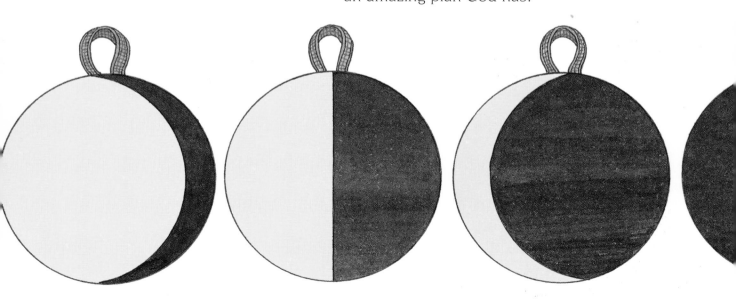

Thank you, God, for the moon.

God made the stars in the night sky.

Star Hair Snaps

you need:

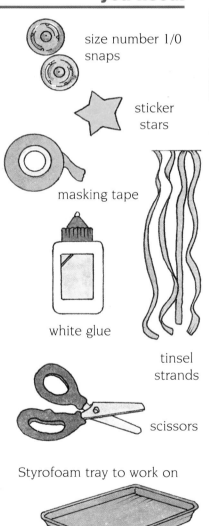

size number 1/0 snaps

sticker stars

masking tape

white glue

tinsel strands

scissors

Styrofoam tray to work on

what you do:

1 Cover the flat topside of a snap with a tiny piece of masking tape to create a better gluing surface. Glue a sticker star over the tape on the snap.

3 Use markers to color a beak on the point and draw on eyes.

4 Glue on two small feather fluffs for wings. Add some snips of feather to the back of the bird for the tail.

To fly the bird, slide the bird over the end of the straw. Aim the bird skyward and blow hard in the other end of the straw.

Thank you, God, for the birds.

God made so many different kinds of birds!

Necktie Bird Finger Puppet

you need:

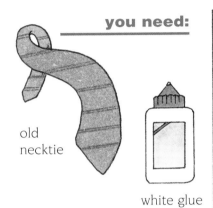

old necktie

white glue

two small wiggle eyes

felt scraps

craft feather

scissors

what you do:

1 Cut a 4-inch (10-cm) piece off the thin end of a necktie. If the seam has come undone in the back, glue it back together.

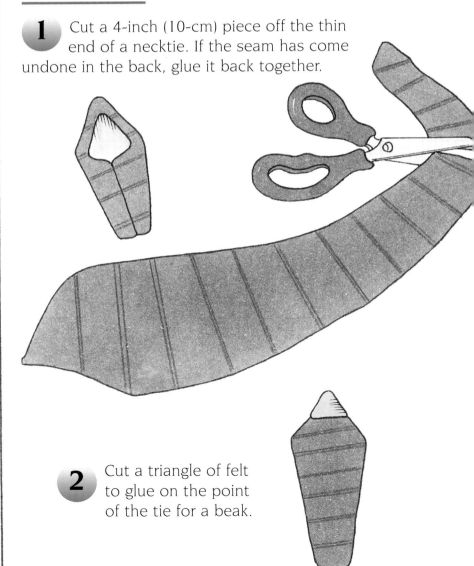

2 Cut a triangle of felt to glue on the point of the tie for a beak.

3 Glue on two eyes above the beak.

4 Fold a piece of felt in half and cut a wing shape on the fold. Open the folded felt so you have two identical wings attached at the center. Glue the center of the wings across the bird.

5 Glue a feather sticking off the back of the bird for a tail.

Make a whole flock of different color birds
. . . one for each finger!

Thank you, God, for so many different birds.

God filled the waters with fish and other creatures.

Bottom of the Sea Diorama

you need:

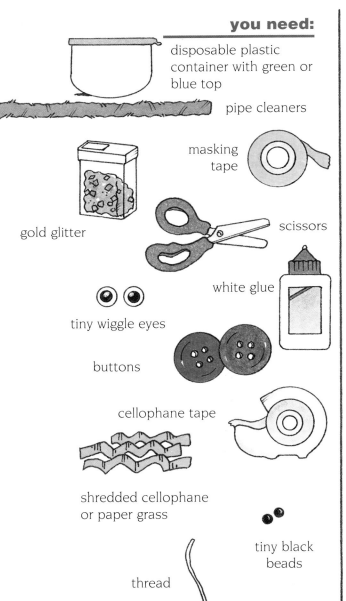

disposable plastic container with green or blue top

pipe cleaners

masking tape

gold glitter

scissors

white glue

tiny wiggle eyes

buttons

cellophane tape

shredded cellophane or paper grass

tiny black beads

thread

what you do:

1 Cut a 3-inch (8-cm) piece of green pipe cleaner. Wrap smaller pieces of pipe cleaner around the pipe cleaner piece to make a seaweed plant. Bend an inch of the bottom of the plant to the side and use masking tape to secure it to the bottom of the container.

2 Cover the bottom of the inside of the container with glue. Sprinkle the glue with gold glitter to look like the sandy ocean bottom.

3 Glue some grass to one side of the container for a different kind of seaweed.

3 Shape the red pipe cleaner into a circle about 1 1/2 inches (3.75 cm) across for a collar for the dog. Remove the head to slip the collar over the middle finger. It should hang loose.

4 Shape two pointed or floppy ears for the dog from the black pipe cleaners. Poke an ear into each side of the head.

5 Put a small piece of masking tape on the back of each wiggle eye to create a better gluing surface. Glue the two eyes on the front of the head.

6 Glue the two larger brown pom-poms on the head below the eyes for the muzzle. Glue the black pom-pom on the end of the muzzle for the nose.

Put your hand in the glove body and secure the head on the end of your finger. Now take the dog for a walk.

Thank you, God, for animals that like to live with people.

God made all the people.

Row of People

you need:

cardboard egg carton

poster paints in six bright colors and a paintbrush

poster paints in six skin tones

12 beads and/or wiggle eyes

six tiny pom-poms

white glue

red marker

buttons

yarn bits in different hair colors

six 12-inch (30-cm) pipe cleaners

ribbon for bow

masking tape

scissors

newspaper to work on

what you do:

1 Cut the lid off the top of the egg carton. Paint the outside of the lid for the "people" to sit on.

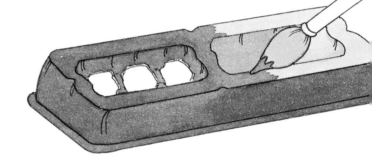

2 Turn the bottom part of the egg carton over. The top row of bumps will be the heads for the people, and the bottom row the bodies. Paint each bump in the top row a different skin tone. Paint each bump in the bottom row a different bright color.

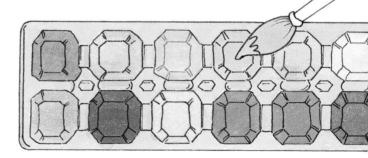

3 Glue two wiggle eyes or beads on each face. Glue on a pom-pom below each pair of eyes for the nose. Use the red marker to give each person a smile. Glue different color yarn bits on the top of each head for hair.

4 Decorate each body by gluing on a bow or button.

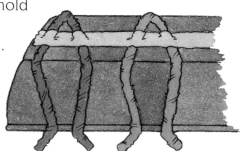

5 Fold each of the six pipe cleaners in half to form legs. Bend the ends to make feet. Glue the folded ends of the pipe-cleaner legs along the lid of the egg carton. Use masking tape to hold the legs in place while the glue is drying. Bend the legs down over the front of the carton to make knees.

6 Glue the people across the lid of the carton over the legs so that each person has a pair of legs sticking out from the body.

Isn't it amazing how different each person is?

Thank you, God, for all the different people.

God made so many different people!

Different People Envelopes Puzzle

you need:

eight or more used white envelopes with nothing written on the back

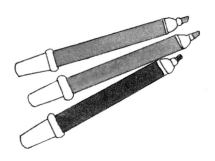

what you do:

1 Line up four different envelopes, unwritten-on side up, one below the other. Draw a head on the top envelope. On the second envelope draw the upper body, as a continuation of the first drawing. On the third envelope draw the lower body portion in pants or a skirt. On the last envelope draw the legs and feet.

2 Remove the head envelope and replace it with a fresh one. Draw a different head on this one, but make it line up with the upper body below it. Do the same thing with each of the other envelopes. You can make as many different envelope pieces as you want, making sure each piece lines up with the original drawing.

3 Add details and color all the different parts with markers.

Have fun making lots of different-looking people by trying different combinations of envelope parts.

Thank you, God, for making each of us in your image.

God made you.

Label Necklace

you need:

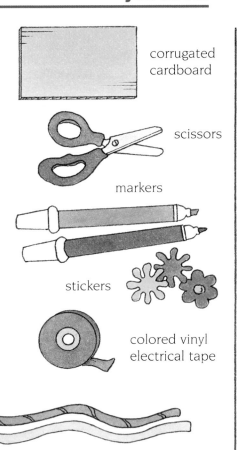

corrugated cardboard

scissors

markers

stickers

colored vinyl electrical tape

thin ribbon or yarn

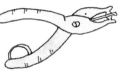

hole punch

what you do:

1 Cut a 5- by 7-inch (13- by 18-cm) piece of corrugated cardboard. Snip off the corners at one end to make it look like a tag. Round off all the corners.

2 Use the markers to write, "Made with love by GOD" on one side of the tag. Decorate the tag any way you want using markers and stickers.

3 Use the electrical tape to make a border for the tag.

4 Punch a hole in the center of the end of the tag with the trimmed corners.

5 Cut a 2-foot (60-cm) length of ribbon. Thread one end of the ribbon through the hole in the tag and tie the two ends together to make a necklace.

You can wear the label as a reminder that you come from God.

Thank you, God, for making me.

God loves the world.

Cross Pin

you need:

eight small gold
safety pins

seed beads in
two colors (make
sure the openings
are large enough
to string on
safety pins)

what you do:

1 Open one safety pin and put on seed beads of one color, then close the safety pin to hold them in place. It will take about eight beads. Because pins can vary, the number of beads needed might vary too, but the idea will still work. Do the same thing with the second safety pin.

2 On the next four safety pins put on four beads of the same color as the first two safety pins, then one bead of the second color, then three more beads of the first color. Close each safety pin to hold the beads in place.

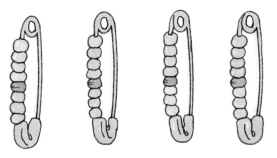

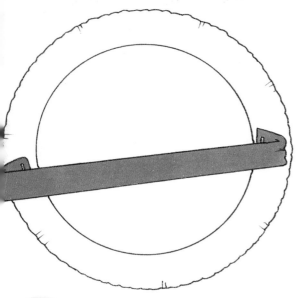

3 Hold the rim up to your face and wrap the rim around your head to make a band to hold the mask in place. Staple the strip to the other side of the rim and trim off any excess paper.

4 Fold the second sheet of paper in half to get a piece that is 9 by 12 inches (23 by 30 cm). Cut half a heart on the fold of the paper, making it as large as the paper will allow. Open up the paper to get a complete heart shape.

5 Place the plate rim on one side of the heart. The plate should not show from the front of the heart. If a tiny part of the plate shows at the top of the heart, just snip off that piece of plate. Trace around the hole in the plate on the heart. Cut the hole out of the heart.

6 Write on the top of the heart, "God Loves . . . " Decorate your heart any way you like, using stickers and/or markers.

7 Glue the heart to the front of the plate rim.

Wear your mask to show everyone that you know that God loves you.

Thank you, God, for loving me.

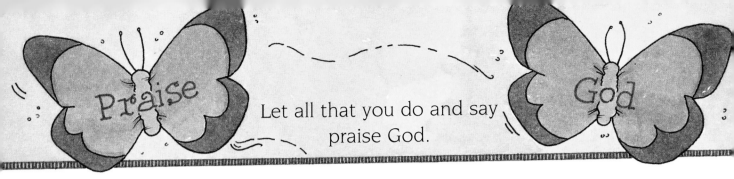

Let all that you do and say praise God.

Praise Puppet

you need:

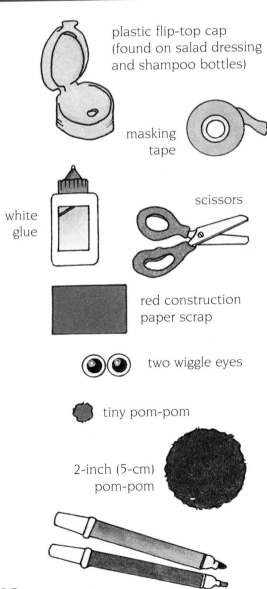

plastic flip-top cap (found on salad dressing and shampoo bottles)

masking tape

white glue

scissors

red construction paper scrap

two wiggle eyes

tiny pom-pom

2-inch (5-cm) pom-pom

markers

what you do:

1 Turn the cap upside-down. The top of the cap will form the bottom jaw of the puppet. Cover the outside of the cap with masking tape. You can use the masking tape shade for the skin color, or use markers to make the skin another color.

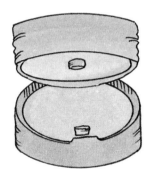

2 Trace around the cap on the red paper. Cut the circle out. Use a marker to write "Praise God" on the circle. Put a piece of masking tape on the inside of the bottom jaw to create a better gluing surface. Glue the circle inside the mouth of the puppet.